Object in Focus

CW00958174

The Lacock Cup
Lloyd de Beer and Naomi Speakman

The British Museum

Contents

Prologue

Cups and drinking vessels are both the most personal and public of objects. The practice of having a favourite mug, or saving the best glasses for special occasions, is something easily recognizable to us. In the Middle Ages drinking vessels could be made for everyday use in humble materials, or could be incredibly ornate and made of precious metal. The Lacock Cup, made in the fifteenth century from plain and gilded silver, is a rare and exquisite example of a drinking vessel which reveals the prestige, wealth and conviviality of medieval dining amongst the elite. It is an object with a unique and fascinating history. In its 500-year lifespan, it has journeyed from the nobleman's table to become an important feature of religious ceremony in the parish church of Lacock, Wiltshire, the village from which it derives its name. During this time, the Cup has witnessed pivotal events that have undoubtedly shaped the European past. This book will tell the story of a magnificent object which has bridged the divide between the religious and secular, and survived the centuries against the odds.

Status and display

Standing at 35 cm in height, the Lacock Cup is comprised of two parts: the base, with bowl and foot, and a sweeping lid (fig. 1). Hammered sheet silver forms the bowl, foot and lid. These sections were soldered together, joined by moulded decorative elements in a crown-like crenellation around the lid, stem and foot. The Cup was made for the sharing of wine; measuring 14 cm in diameter, the bowl was clearly designed to hold a significant amount of liquid. Cups of this style were typical of the fifteenth century, and were popular in the late Middle Ages, as can be seen from examples depicted in stained glass and manuscript illuminations (see figs 18–19). Medieval wills list cups like this in a variety of ways including 'hanaps', 'stonnynge', 'bells' and 'bolepeces'.

The Lacock Cup's decoration might at first seem simple, though the goldsmith has used plain silver and gilding to create contrasts in shape and colour. Great technical skill was required to form the smooth hammered surface, and the exaggerated curves of the lid, bowl and foot, which dramatically reflect the light. The elements of gilding, in bright gold bands, highlight areas of the Cup and add to the brilliant shine on the vessel's surface. In addition the moulded designs are cast, gilded and have an openwork design. The Cup is a showpiece, designed to stand out and to be seen from afar. The lid is a case in point; when removed and placed alongside the Cup, it appears to be nearly the same height as the base itself (fig. 2). When the lid is replaced it doubles the height of the Cup, and topped with a gilded sphere and finial it cannot fail to draw the eye. The Cup has been virtually unaltered since its manufacture and is in extremely good condition. Compared with contemporary imagery, it appears today as if the Cup had just emerged from the goldsmith's workshop.

Cups in the Bible

In order to fully appreciate the importance of the Lacock Cup in medieval England, we must consider the role cups performed in society at the time. Standing cups and drinking vessels were extremely popular in the Middle Ages at every level of society. Cups, particularly of precious metal, had great symbolic importance due to their reference in the Bible and their role in the Mass. In the Bible, cups are associated with strong emotions, with God's judgment and anger, or with blessing and salvation, and feature in numerous biblical stories. Many will recall that in Genesis 44:2, Joseph (with his multicoloured coat) hides a silver cup in young Benjamin's grain sack. In Jeremiah 51:7, the ancient city of Babylon is described as a gold cup which has made the earth drunk. The act of drinking and sharing wine is a common biblical motif, from Christ's first miracle transforming water into wine at the Marriage at Cana, to the wine becoming Christ's blood at the Last Supper. The symbolic resonance of cups in both biblical and secular stories would not have been lost on a medieval audience: the Arthurian legend, which centres on the search for the Holy Grail, would have been well known.

For royal occasions

Just as cups and drinking feature heavily in the Bible, so drinking vessels were central to great social occasions. Drinking cups were used at royal coronations in the fifteenth century: cups used at the coronation feasts of Edward IV (r. 1461–70 and 1471–83) and Richard III (r. 1483–85) were bequeathed by Sir William Alington to his son in 1485. But it was not only at grand state events that treasured vessels were used. Religious festivals could also feature a special cup. In 1406 William Carent of Montacute left his son, 'one horn with cover of silver and gilt in which I was accustomed to drink at the Feast of the Nativity of our Lord'.

As with the royal examples, which sadly have not survived, grand drinking cups were often associated with certain people or places. Many of those that have survived are owned by the colleges in the universities of Oxford and Cambridge and are associated with a particular donor. For example, the colleges of Trinity Hall, Cambridge and Oriel College, Oxford, both own medieval drinking vessels which traditionally have been associated with their founders. Christ's College and Pembroke College, Cambridge, both own medieval drinking cups known as 'Foundress's Cups'. The cup owned by Christ's College was donated by Lady Margaret Beaufort, the mother of Henry VII (r. 1485–1509), and bears the arms of Humphrey Duke of Gloucester (1390–1447), the youngest son of Henry IV (r. 1399–1413) and his second wife Eleanor of Cobham (figs 3 and 4). This cup shares stylistic similarities with the Lacock Cup: a similar shape of foot, bowl and lid; the twisted motif around the rim; and the spherical knop on top of the lid. The decoration on the Cambridge cup, by contrast with that on the Lacock Cup, marks it out as a particularly costly work – understandable given it was a royal gift. It seems evident therefore that in the hierarchy of the small number of surviving examples, the Lacock Cup was most likely made for the gentry or nobility, rather than for royalty.

4. Detail of enamelled plaque from the Foundress's Cup (see fig. 3) showing the arms of Humphrey Duke of Gloucester and his second wife Eleanor of Cobham. Reproduced by kind permission of the Master and Fellows of Christ's College, Cambridge.

5. The Royal Gold Cup. Gold and enamel, France, mid 14th century (see also p. 35). Height 23.6 cm; diameter 17.8 cm. British Museum 1892,0501.1. Acquired with contributions from the HM Treasury, The Worshipful Company of Goldsmiths, Sir Augustus Wollaston Franks and others.

Precious vessels

Few secular dining vessels survive from the late Middle Ages with which to compare the Lacock Cup. At the upper end of the spectrum is the exquisite Royal Gold Cup rendered in gold and enamel for the French royal family in *c*.1370–1380 (fig. 5). Far more utilitarian, but still splendid, is the mazer: a bowl carved in maple wood, decorated with silver or silver-gilt mounts, such as the Flemish example in the British Museum, which dates from the fifteenth century (fig. 6). The mazer bowl and lid itself are low and round, turned so that they slot together. On top of the lid is a silver-gilt bird, around whose neck is hung a shield with the arms of Flanders, now the northern part of Belgium. The foot of the bowl is of a similar trumpet shape to that of the Lacock Cup, and is decorated with enamelled panels repeating the bird and suspended shield motif. This example is clearly very refined, yet mazers were not just the reserve of the nobility. In 1493 one wealthy York tanner, Robert Allerton, left his son John a number of silver items including 'the best mazer'. It is perhaps because of their composite parts that more mazers survive than any other type of drinking vessel.

10

Their wooden elements were not precious and so they were less likely to be broken up for remodelling, or have their silver parts melted down for their bullion value. Other types of drinking cup included those made of coconut shells, with precious metal mounts, which combined the exotic with the practical. Like mazers they were less likely to be broken up than vessels made entirely of silver. Coconut cups could carry both religious and secular messages. One such cup, dating from the fifteenth century and in the collection of New College, Oxford, is inscribed with 'Ave Maria' (Hail Mary in Latin). Drinking horns, popular in Anglo-Saxon England continued in use throughout the medieval period. Surviving medieval examples are often inventively given

birdlike clawed feet, so that the twisted horn appears to stand proud, adding a playful touch to the dinner table (fig. 7). Cups also survive in less precious materials such as wood and ceramics, further emphasizing that they were used by all levels of medieval society.

The inscriptions on such surviving vessels reveal the joy and fun to be had in drinking from them. For example, the Founders Cup, from Pembroke College, Oxford, bears a playful inscription, which bids the holder to 'mak gud cher' (make good cheer). A drinking horn from Queen's College, Oxford – which was reputed to have been given by Philippa of Hainault, wife of Edward III (r. 1327–77), although this is now not believed to be true – is inscribed three times with 'WASSEYL', a version of the Old English drinking salutation, *wassail*. These vessels could also bestow blessings, or display protective messages. A mazer bowl at the British Museum which dates from *c.*1490, is engraved in Latin and Greek asking 'May the Holy One bless the drink and us'.

Material and manufacture

The Lacock Cup is formed from nearly 1 kilogram of silver. This precious metal has long been a medium of exchange and wealth, and formed a cornerstone of medieval coinage. The quality of silver and gold was tightly protected in medieval England, as today, and the silver standard was maintained at 92.5%. The grandest objects were crafted in gold, such as the Royal Gold Cup (fig. 5), but silver was more commonly used because it was more hard-wearing, more affordable and yet still very fine, and so it attained a great deal of importance in medieval society. The importance of silver, and silver working, was emphasized in the Bible, and the material is frequently mentioned in relation to purification and redemption. In Malachi 3:3, God is described as 'a refiner and purifier of silver, and he will purify the sons of Levi and refine them like gold and silver.'

A fine investment

At a time when there were no banks, silver objects such as dishes, cutlery and drinking vessels were tangible forms of investment which advertised material wealth. Silver was a public display of a person's resources and could be easily melted down for its bullion value whenever ready cash was needed. The Lacock Cup, with its bands of gilding and sheets of hammered silver, positively shines with wealth. Because of this bullion value, secular silver objects from the Middle Ages could become currency in themselves, and for this reason the survival of the Lacock Cup is all the more extraordinary. The Cup most likely survived in private hands and would have been seen as a ready source of instant money had the owner needed it. A fine example of silver used in this way is provided in an undated letter, thought to be written between 1200–1250, from the Earl of Gloucester to his draper in London regarding unpaid bills for cloth. The Earl begs to secure credit for an order of fabric by sending a pledge 'upon the ten gold rings and ten silver cups that we send you.' Silver cups could be used as another form of payment, as many medieval wills gift their executors' cups, and other silver objects, as surety that they will carry out their last wishes. The will of an Edith Gaskin, from December 1457, leaves to a Sir Henry Hayne, 'one small cup covered and gilt, with that intent, that he be one of the executors of this my will'. Conversely, aside from the destruction of silver, these objects were also amassed by wealthy medieval society to ensure and display one's wealth. One of the most famous figures of this is the well-documented Sir John Fastolf, who, upon his death in 1459, had over 13,000 ounces of silver in his mansion at Caister, Norfolk. Medieval owners of silver took great pains to keep their collections safe. In large houses silver vessels were kept in the buttery, a service room with the principal function of storing and serving wine. A fifteenth-century royal ordinance of Edward IV lists that the buttery was divided, and that one part was turned into a space dedicated to the storage of cups. At the Palace of Westminster the Jewel Tower was the repository for the royal collection of silver and gold: it had a resident administrator and was within view of the palace.

Great chests were also used to keep silver safe, with more than one key holder required to unlock the complex locks.

But silver was much more than an investment: it was a precious material in its own right. Fantastical and whimsical objects were sometimes made of silver. Piers Gaveston, the companion of Edward II (r. 1307–27), is listed in 1313 as owning a ship, also known as a *nef*, wrought in silver on four wheels and the previously mentioned inventory of Sir John Fastolf lists gilded silver cups which looked like fountains, decorated with flowers and pearls. We also find some surprising objects fashioned in silver; the collection belonging to the Paston family in 1479 includes a tiny egg spoon, while the French Count Amadeus of Savoy bought a silver urinal when visiting London in 1292.

Fewer than 300 pieces of English silverware survive from before 1520: a very poor rate given that King John of England (r. 1199–1216) alone owned some 157 cups and goblets and 8 flagons. Silver was passed on as heirlooms, although texts rarely provide identifiable details, and old silver was often remodelled or melted down to create new pieces, which could in part explain the loss of so many items. Pieces could be altered to make them more fashionable, or to update them into different contexts. A fine medieval example can be found in the Palais de Tau, Rheims, France, and takes the form of a silver ship (fig. 8). This vessel was originally a secular object given to Queen Anne de Bretagne (Duchess of Brittany, r.1488–1514) by the aldermen of Tours to celebrate her entry into the city in 1500. Its lid, which is designed as the bridge of a ship, was decorated with miniature courtiers and soldiers. A few years later, the queen had the piece turned into a holy reliquary by replacing the figures with Saint Ursula and her virgin handmaids, rendered in gold and silver.

Gilding

The gilding of silver objects was common practice in the medieval world, and pieces could be entirely or partially gilded (parcel-gilt), depending on the amount the client

was willing to spend. The Lacock Cup is no different and is beautifully gilded in parts, with bands of reflective gold. Gilding was a more affordable, and still an extremely grand way to give silver and base metal vessels a golden appearance. The most commonly-used technique was mercury gilding, whereby mercury and gold were mixed together and applied to the surface of the object. When heated the mercury evaporated leaving a gilded surface. A French or German drinking cup at the British Museum, dating from the same century as the Lacock Cup appears to be made in gold. However, closer inspection reveals a silver surface, which has been entirely gilded in tissue-thin gold, known as gold leaf (fig. 9). Marian Campbell, an expert on medieval metalwork, has noted that in the Middle Ages goldsmiths often obtained the gold for gold leaf and gilding from foreign coins. As with the purity and working of gold and silver, the process of gilding was also regulated. This was important as the gilding covered up the underlying metal which could have been precious or base (one that oxidizes or corrodes easily). A statute issued in 1404 under Henry IV (r. 1399–1413) permitted liturgical vessels in base metal to be gilded, but this was forbidden for secular items.

The goldsmith

'In one single street…leading to St Paul's there are 52 goldsmiths' shops so rich and full of silver vessels, great and small, that in all the shops in Milan, Rome, Venice and Florence put together I do not think there would be found so many of the magnificence…to be seen in London. And these vessels are all either salt cellars, or drinking cups, or basins to hold water for the hands.'
Milanese visitor to London, c.1500

This Milanese visitor was writing about Cheapside in the City of London, which for many years was an epicentre of the English goldsmiths' trade. A lack of makers' marks for this period means it is impossible to say where the Lacock Cup was made, though it could conceivably have originated from a London goldsmith. The 52 goldsmiths' shops lining

9. Drinking cup. Silver-gilt, France or Germany, 15th century. Height 12.3 cm. British Museum AF.3048. Bequeathed by Sir Augustus Wollaston Franks.

Cheapside indicate a bustling and active market, which we can see in the detail from the Coronation Procession of Edward VI in 1547 (fig. 10). Standing cups of many styles are displayed in the open windows of the shops above the heads of the mounted procession.

Although they were recorded in London earlier than the fourteenth century, the goldsmiths received their royal charter in 1327. The Worshipful Company of Goldsmiths was responsible for regulating the trade, and for testing the quality of gold and silver, which is known as assaying. During the period when the Lacock Cup was made, this process of assaying would have made use of a touchstone,

used to test the purity of the metal content (fig. 11). Silver
purity was tested by rubbing a small portion of the silver
from the finished object onto the touchstone. The resulting
marks were compared to those produced by rubbing a piece
of silver of a known purity on the same stone. There were
also regional centres for metalwork. In the Statutes of 1423,
seven towns in addition to London are established as assay
towns: York, Newcastle-upon-Tyne, Lincoln, Norwich,
Bristol, Salisbury and Coventry. The Leopard's Head Mark
was the hallmark for London, and is recorded in the 1327
charter, and one of the earliest surviving objects bearing the
mark is the Shrewsbury bowl, which dates to c.1350–1400,
now at Rowley's House Museum in Shrewsbury. Very few
surviving medieval pieces have hallmarks of any kind,
including the Lacock Cup. This suggests that the process
of hallmarking was perhaps a piecemeal one, and only

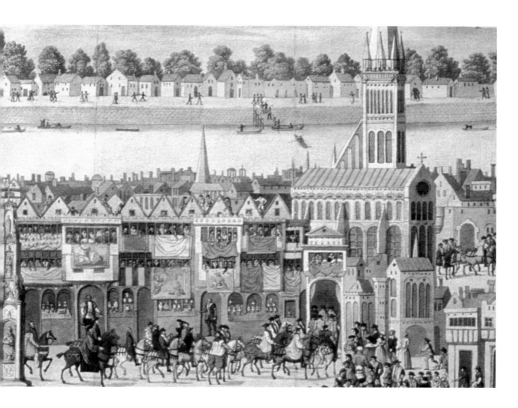

undertaken early on when there was a need to validate the quality of the silver. The mark came into practice to protect purchasers of silver from being misled into buying material of lower quality. Recent testing of the silver composition of the Lacock Cup reveals that the hammered metal ranges in purity between 91% and 98%, indicating a high quality of silver that is broadly in keeping with the silver standard.

There is not a great deal of remaining physical evidence for the goldsmith's working practice and equipment in Medieval England. In common with goldsmiths of later periods, the techniques and tools perfected by the artist were protected so as to not give away the secrets of manufacture. Two descriptions of twelfth- and thirteenth-century goldsmiths provide insight into workshop practice. Alexander Neckam (1157–1217) described the twelfth century goldsmith and his workshop in *De Nominibus*

11. Touchstone used to test the purity of gold and silver. Black limestone, Flanders, c.1500–1600. Length 5.6 cm. British Museum 1870,1228.1. Donated by Robert Boyd.

Utensilium. Jean de Garlande in his *Dictionarius* of Parisian goldsmiths, from the 1220s, also described their methods, 'The goldsmiths sit before their furnaces and tables on the Grand-Pont and make hanaps of gold and silver and brooches and bracelets and pins and buttons, and choose garnets and jasper, sapphires and emeralds for rings.' (Hanap was another term used for a drinking cup, and appears in inventories of the period.) Artistic representations provide further information on medieval metalworking techniques. Saint Eligius, the patron saint of goldsmiths, is commonly depicted in his workshop, surrounded by the tools of his craft. His tale appears in William Caxton's English printed edition of the Golden Legend in which he was called St Loye, (although the tale doesn't feature in Jacobus Voragine's original published in the late thirteenth century). According to the legend, Eligius [Loye] 'knew well the craft and art of goldsmithery' and proved his skill by making the king of France two gold and gem-encrusted saddles. Niclaus Manuel's painting of *Saint Eligius at Work*, dated 1515, opens a window into these workshops (fig. 12). Among the silver and gold items we find beakers, chalices and cups, with one man working on a gold ring. Among the tools are chisels, a hammer, a clamp and drill bits. In the background on the right a small figure pumps the bellows of the fire, which illuminate his face. Even Saint Eligius' halo appears as a finely worked golden dish.

The drinking cup and the goldsmith were intrinsically linked. Granted in 1571, the coat of arms of the London Company of Goldsmith's contains two standing covered cups, each between two buckles, quartered with the leopard's head, symbolizing the assay mark. Drinking vessels were also used to represent goldsmiths in other media. A thirteenth-century seal matrix, used to impress a seal in wax, from the British Museum, is thought to have belonged to a goldsmith (fig. 13). The image at the centre is a standing cup or mazer, and the legend round the edge of the matrix reads *S'WILLI DE DUNTONE, 'The Seal of William Dunton'. William Dunton may well have been an English goldsmith working in the second half of the thirteenth century, who used the image of the drinking cup to represent his craft and trade. Further afield, the silver vessel was used by other goldsmiths in their seal matrices. The silver seal matrix of the Estonian goldsmiths from Tallinn, *c.*1500, contains a small shield decorated with a tiny double drinking cup, an example of which is held in the Victoria and Albert Museum in London.

12. *Saint Eligius at Work.* Oil on wood. Niclaus Manuel, 1515. 120.5 x 83.3 cm. Kunstmuseum, Bern.

13. Seal matrix of William Dunton showing a standing cup or mazer. Copper alloy, England, 1250–1300. Diameter 1.9 cm. British Museum 1996,0401.8.

The Lord's table

'The cup should be held between two fingers;
The thumb should not touch the sweet wine…
Drink and then turn the bowl to thy neighbor,
So that his lips are not placed where thine were'
De doctrina morum, probably early 15ᵗʰ century

The rituals of display and dining are ways of marking social distinctions in many world cultures. The Lacock Cup was designed with the dining traditions of late medieval Europe in mind. Precious and splendid, it was quite clearly destined for the table of nobility, and its large bowl was made for sharing wine. Contemporary accounts and images detail this practice. A manuscript illumination of a private feast at Nuremberg, Germany on 8th December 1523 shows five expensively dressed diners, each clearly with their own place settings and knives ready to receive their food (fig. 14). Set out before them are two standing cups, to be shared by the five diners. As it was the responsibility of the host to provide the cups, this principle of sharing was surely a sign of his status and ability to provide. The shapes of the drinking vessels shown in this illumination are quite similar to that of the Lacock Cup.

25

14. Private feast in Nuremberg on 8th December 1523. From Prince Arthur's book, College of Arms, Ms. Vincent 152, f.178.

15. Mazer bowl. Maple wood, silver-gilt, England, c.1470. Diameter 14.7 cm; height 5.7 cm. British Museum 1909,0624.1.

A culture of sharing wine from one cup can be seen in the example of Grace or Loving cups, which would be passed around the table at the end of a meal, while a traditional prayer of thanksgiving was said. We can learn about such shared grace and other dining practices and etiquette from the inscriptions on the rims of drinking vessels such as these. For example, a mazer from c.1470 at the British Museum is encircled with the inscription, translated from Latin, 'I ask Christ to bless the vessel and the drink' (fig. 15). The opening quotation to this chapter, taken from a fifteenth-century text on table manners, outlines the way a diner should pass on the cup to their neighbour, so that no drinker sips from the side which has just been drunk from. The etiquette of medieval dining was tightly controlled, particularly at the higher levels of society, where hugely elaborate feasts often took place. For example, the Duke of Buckingham hosted a Christmas Day dinner in 1507 for 294 people. At such an event, the order in which guests sat at table, which was defined by their rank, was especially important. The Rokewode Mazer, from the Victoria and Albert Museum, offers perhaps the wisest guidance on how to behave appropriately during a meal. The inscription reads, 'Hold your tongue and say the best, and let your neighbour sit in rest, whoso listeth god to please, let his neighbor live in ease'.

Setting the table

Traditionally drinking cups would have been placed in front of the most important diners at the table alongside the ceremonial salt cellar, which was placed to the right of the most important guest. Wynkin de Worde's *Boke of Kervynge*, written in 1508 instructs, 'set your salt on the right side where your soverayne shall sytte…and at every end of the table set a salte seller.' The salt cellar was given prominence on the table since the salt was seen to represent the concord between God and man, and the cellar itself represented God's presence at the table. Salts from the Middle Ages are among the most dramatic and elaborate dining objects to have survived. Although they commonly had grand proportions, they hold a surprisingly small cavity for the salt, since it was an expensive commodity. Warden Hill's salt, at New College, Oxford was given to the college at some point between 1475–94, and is a wondrously ornate example (fig. 16). With a twisted foot in the form of an hour-glass, a crenellated edging and an architectural lid, it bears some resemblance to the Lacock Cup.

Diners would bring their own cutlery to a meal, but cups, salt cellars and salvers (flat trays used for carrying or serving glasses, cups and dishes) would be supplied by the host. The host's outlets for demonstrating his wealth, and refined taste, were therefore through salts and cups. The fact that they were not required to be routinely carried to different locations meant they could be large and elaborate. When not in use, they would be displayed at the side of the hall on a buffet, so that they were permanently on show. Diners could also contribute demonstrations of their wealth at the table. A delicately enamelled travelling spoon from the British Museum would have been an elegant addition to any meal (fig. 17). The spoon, from fifteenth-century Burgundy, is formed in three parts: the bowl, the stem, and the end of the stem with a finial. These sections would screw together, and fit into their original leather travelling case. The spoon is gilded silver, and the bowl is enamelled with green foliage, and the script 'Ave Maria' echoes the blessings found inscribed on drinking vessels. Diners would also bring their own knives, which were carried in pouches attached to

28

the belt. In a stained glass roundel dating from *c*.1450–75
from a series of the Labours of the Months, December is
rendered as a king seated before a richly dressed table with
two companions. His table-setting demonstrates how a
medieval table would have been arranged (fig. 18). Before
him are placed two grand standing cups, topped by lids
resembling the crown worn by the central figure. In addition
to the cups are beakers, plates and a knife with a golden
handle. The Labours of the Months were an agricultural
calendar, depicting different seasonal activities such as
harvesting and threshing. However at the end of the year,
the months of December and January were dedicated
to feasting. It is interesting that contemporary images of
feasting, such as this roundel, have at their very centre
standing cups which resemble the Lacock Cup. Perhaps

then, for a medieval viewer, an image of a standing cup could readily denote dining and splendour.

The *Adoration of the Magi* is another important and often depicted event in which the standing cup took centre stage. The Three Kings, or Magi, were some of the most popular and widely referenced religious figures in the Middle Ages. Caspar, Balthazar and Melchior were the original pilgrims and an example to all pious Christians of the culture of gift-giving. Their relics were held at Cologne, Germany, where what was claimed to be their three skulls have been enshrined within the cathedral since they were given to the Archbishop of Cologne in 1164. The three gifts of the Magi were gold, frankincense and myrrh; and in medieval images of the presentation of these gifts it is the gift of gold which is frequently the first offering presented to the infant

Christ, sometimes within a golden cup. A panel of stained glass in the east window of the church of St Peter Mancroft, Norwich, dating from the middle of the fifteenth century, depicts the Three Magi's Adoration of the Virgin Mary (fig. 19). There are two standing cups imaged in this scene, which bear close resemblance to the Lacock Cup. Before the Virgin and Child a thickly-bearded King kneels and opens his cup to reveal that it is filled with gold. He holds this cup above his crown which he has placed before the Virgin and Christ.

This symbolic declaration in front of the Christ child creates a link between the metal in the cup and the purity of Christ in infancy. The king standing the furthest back, holds another cup in his hands, which Christ gazes at directly.

19. Stained glass panel showing the Adoration of the Magi, England, c.1455–60. Church of St Peter Mancroft, Norwich. Photo © Alamy.

The purity of the material of the standing cup, and its connection with royalty and nobility, makes this an entirely suitable object to be presented by the Magi to Christ. This holy connection was one acknowledged by goldsmiths on the vessels themselves. Two mazers, one from the church of the Holy Trinity, Colchester, which dates to c.1480, and another late fourteenth century one known as the 'Swan Mazer', from Corpus Christi College, Cambridge, both have mounts inscribed with the names of the Magi. Guilds of goldsmiths also publicly associated themselves with the Three Kings, undertaking performances dedicated to them. In 1455, the goldsmiths of Beverley in Yorkshire arranged to perform, with other guilds in the city, a yearly pageant of the Three Kings.

It is clear then that standing cups in precious metal took on a number of roles in the Middle Ages: as a key element in formal dining and social rituals of feasting and gift-giving; as representations of wealth; as symbols of kings and of the goldsmith's craft; and as a gift to place before the infant Christ.

Surviving the odds

Up until now, we have looked only at the Lacock Cup as a splendid piece of dining silver on the medieval nobleman's table. But it is rare that objects of great age and antiquity retain their original use for long. It can also sometimes be difficult to discern their intended function. The Royal Gold Cup is a case in point. It was probably commissioned by Jean Duc de Berry for his brother Charles V, King of France (r. 1364–80). Charles however died before he could receive it and it instead passed into the hands of his successor Charles VI (r. 1380–1422). From him it passed to John Duke of Bedford, brother of Henry V (r. 1413–22), and into English royal ownership. Henry VIII (r. 1509–47) added a gold band to the stem of the Cup, introducing a new statement of ownership through the decoration of enamelled red and white Tudor roses (fig. 20). The Cup stayed in the English Royal Treasury through the sixteenth century until it was included in an exchange of gifts as part of the Treaty of London, which was signed at Somerset House in 1604. To commemorate this important peace treaty with Spain after decades of war, gifts of gold and silver were given by James VI (of Scotland) & I (King of England, 1603–25) as peace pledges. Juan De Velasco, Constable of Castile, was the principal peace envoy on behalf of Phillip III of Spain. He was given the Royal Gold Cup by James I, and added a gold band to the foot with an inscription in Latin recording its value as, 'a memorial to the peace made between the kings…given to Christ the Peacemaker by Juan de Velasco'. In 1610 he donated the Cup to the convent in Medina de Pomar, Burgos, for liturgical use. The nuns owned the Cup until the late nineteenth century, and in 1883 it was released for sale in Paris by a private dealer. The Cup was subsequently purchased by the first Keeper of the department of British Antiquities, Sir Augustus Wollaston Franks, through subscription and it has remained at the British Museum ever since. The Royal Gold Cup is a significant example of the practice of gifting secular cups to religious institutions as symbolic gestures. In the inscription on the Cup, De Velasco links the Cup to the peace between Great Britain and Spain, and then gifts it to Christ, marking his presence in its actions and uses.

Although we are able to construct a history for the Royal Gold Cup through royal inventories and historical documents we are in many ways no closer to understanding its original function, or its possible many uses. It is decorated with religious iconography depicting the martyrdom of Saint Agnes, yet takes the form of a secular drinking cup.

20. Detail of the Royal Gold Cup (see fig. 5), showing the gold band added by Henry VIII.

The enamelled roundel of Christ in the centre of the bowl suggests that it may have functioned as a *ciborium* (a vessel for the sacred host). This has raised some confusion and has provoked debate about the status of the Cup. Perhaps it was never used at all and was rather admired for its great beauty and skill in manufacture, as it is at the Museum today.

The story of the Lacock Cup's survival is no less remarkable than that of the Royal Gold Cup. With so few pieces of pre-1520 secular silver remaining, it must have travelled a journey similar to that of the Royal Gold Cup, wherein it was treasured, admired and protected from external forces which might have brought about its destruction. Given the weight of the Lacock Cup, it could have quite easily been melted down for its value as bullion at any point in its long history, during which time the majority of comparable pieces suffered this fate. The fact that it was never buried, destroyed or melted down for refashioning is a testament to its importance. Whereas the Royal Gold Cup travelled from France to England, to Spain, Paris and back to England, the Lacock Cup most probably remained in England for its entire life, providing a truly national dimension to its history.

A mysterious donation

Exactly how the Cup ventured from the dining table and ended up in the parish church of St Cyriac's in Lacock is still something of a mystery. We do not know precisely when the Cup was given to the church or by whom. It is first described in nineteenth-century catalogues of church silver and was illustrated in a survey of the silver plate in Wiltshire in 1891 (fig. 21). The 1882 *Handbook for Travellers* in Wiltshire, Dorsetshire and Somersetshire said of Saint Cyriac's Church, 'The sacramental plate includes a *ciborium* now used as the chalice.' The Cup's journey from secular dining vessel to liturgical communion cup was probably carefully calculated.

The chalice in medieval England

Cups have been used in divine ceremonies in many ways throughout history. Christianity evolved and took shape during the decline of the Western Roman Empire after the fourth century AD, and placed a particular emphasis on the cup used during its holiest sacrament, the Eucharist, at the altar. The altar had its roots in the Old Testament and was the place where sacrifices were enacted and repeated for the glory of God. It was at an altar that Abraham was told to sacrifice his son Isaac, and the Book of Leviticus places great importance on the act of sacrifice according to Judeo-

21. The earliest image of the Lacock Cup; from J. E. Nightingale, *The Church Plate of Wiltshire*, 1891.

22. The Mass of St Gregory the Great. Hand-coloured, woodcut print, by an anonymous artist, c.1480–1500. 14.2 x 9.8 cm. British Museum 1845,0724.4.d.

Christian religion. In the Book of Numbers 7:84, after the dedication of the altar, the leaders of Israel bring silver as an offering; twelve silver plates, twelve silver bowls, and twelve silver dishes. The role of the cup, however, is taken from the New Testament, and in particular from the story of the Last Supper in the book of Matthew. At the table Christ takes the cup, gives thanks and then gives it to his disciples saying:

'Drink from it, all of you. This is my blood of the covenant, which is poured out for many for the forgiveness of sins.'

As the Christian religion developed a liturgical structure, the altar and the cup were combined into a ceremony which became the Mass, just as the New Testament and Old Testament were combined to become the Bible. The altar became a place for the symbolic re-enactment of the death and resurrection of Christ, and was where his body and blood in the guise of bread and wine could be prepared for the laity. The chalice shown in the print of the Mass of St Gregory the Great (fig. 22) is very similar to the type of chalice which would have been used in parish churches in England during the fifteenth century (fig. 23). It is also close in date to the Lacock Cup. However the medieval chalice has a smaller bowl and an elongated stem, with a flat base and rounded or spiked knop encircling the centre of the stem. The bases and knops of chalices were often decorated with religious imagery or the arms of a donor. The reason for the disparity in sizes between these two vessels is that the Lacock Cup was filled with wine and shared at a feast, whilst the medieval chalice was designed to hold only enough wine for the celebrant priest. None of this would have been wasted as it was considered to have literally become the blood of Christ through the grace of God during the Mass. The print makes this physical connection between death and salvation apparent with its presentation of Christ, who appears to St Gregory from a tomb placed on the altar. Christ points towards the chalice with his hand, which bears the wounds from his sacrifice on the cross, explicitly connecting the blood in his body to the cup placed on the altar.

The chalice was a central focus for the sacrament of the Mass. However, while the body of Christ could be taken by the laity, the blood of Christ was reserved for the clergy. This ownership of the Mass became

23. Chalice. Copper-gilt, England, c.1480. Height 16.6 cm; diameter 12 cm. © Victoria and Albert Museum, London, M.42-1961.

a particular focus for religious reformers from the fourteenth century onwards.

In most English medieval parishes the preparation and consumption of the blood of Christ was also celebrated from behind a divider, now commonly called a rood screen or chancel screen. This partition divided the main body of the church, the nave, from the area specially reserved for the clergy during the Mass, the chancel. These formal and symbolic spatial distinctions in the church, and the administration of the Mass were vigorously contested in the sixteenth century, and would shape the reasons for the eventual donation of the Lacock Cup to the church of St Cyriac's.

The small remains

The vast majority of English silver which has survived from the medieval period is for liturgical use. A key reason for this is the inclusion of precious objects in burials associated with clergy. William of Blois who held the Bishopric of Worcester in the thirteenth century spoke out in 1229, stating that: 'churches should retain two chalices, one in silver for Mass and another made of tin for burial with the priest'. This advice does not seem to have been followed to the letter, as silver manufactured after this date has been discovered in clerical graves at York, Lincoln, Salisbury and Chester. One of the finest chalices to remain was deposited, with its paten (the small plate used to hold the bread during Mass), in the tomb of the Archbishop of Canterbury, Hubert Walter (d. 1205). Other silver chalices have been excavated adding considerably to our understanding of medieval metalwork. A ninth-century chalice found in the eighteenth century at Trewhiddle, Cornwall, is the only Anglo-Saxon silver chalice currently known to survive from Britain (fig. 24). Other notable archaeological

24. Chalice. Silver-gilt, 9th century, found in Trewhiddle, Cornwall, England. Height 12.6 cm. British Museum 1880,0410.1-3. Donated by John Jope Rogers.

25. Dolgellau Chalice. Silver-gilt, England, c.1230–50. Height 18.3 cm. Royal Collection Trust/© Her Majesty Queen Elizabeth II 2014.

discoveries include the thirteenth-century Dolgellau Chalice, which was found on the mountainside of Cwn Mynach, Wales in 1890 (fig. 25). This chalice is an excellent comparison for two thirteenth-century chalices now at the British Museum, The Noble Chalice of c.1250 (fig. 26), and the c.1200 chalice from Berwick St James. All three share stylistic similarities showing a clear preference for this type of design in religious silverware of the period.

Although there is so little remaining, an argument could be made that secular silver was subject to an ever-changing environment of style and taste and, as has been discussed, could be melted down without consideration to the antiquity of the object. This is not to suggest that contemporary fashions did not affect the church – in many ways the church led in taste – but rather that silver which had been blessed and used in the Mass would have held a different social value and perhaps would have been harder to melt down.

26. The Noble Chalice. Silver-gilt, England, c.1250. Height 14.3 cm; diameter 12.9 cm. British Museum 1968,1206.1. Acquired with contribution from The Art Fund.

27. Pilgrim-badge showing Saint Thomas Becket on horseback. Lead alloy, England, 14th century. Height 9.3 cm; width 7.6 cm. British Museum 1984,0505.1.

During the first half of the sixteenth century the role of the priest, the chalice, the altar and indeed the entire structure of Catholicism would be challenged and the English Church would never be the same again.

The split from Rome

Over the course of the century after its split from Rome in the 1530s, the Church in England underwent a series of changes which would make it almost unrecognizable both in liturgy and ritual to the late medieval Catholic Church. The great monastic foundations of medieval England, which had wielded such power, were suppressed and stripped of their possessions under Henry VIII. This included many of the most important pilgrim shrines in the country such as those of Saint Thomas Becket at Canterbury and The House of Our Lady of Walsingham. These sites were visited in great number by religious travellers from all over England and abroad, and the effect of their suppression would have been felt further afield across Europe (fig. 27). These medieval foundations, some of which dated back to before the Norman invasion of 1066, were great patrons of the arts, both musical and visual. As patrons, the leaders of these institutions commissioned objects of great beauty which were made by artists, of both English and continental origin, who possessed impressive skills. The survival of gold and silver objects from such sites is extremely rare, however some objects did survive, and the gilded bronze morses from Warden Abbey, Bedfordshire are an outstanding reminder of the embellishments of the religious houses (fig. 28). The suppression of monastic sites was led by Henry's Chancellor, Thomas Cromwell, and yielded great financial reward for the crown. It has been suggested that the value of the confiscations of silver and gold could have been in the region of one million pounds, and that the weight of the silver amounted to somewhere near 289,768 oz. It was also recorded that men were working around the clock in the Tower of London to stamp coinage from the confiscated silver.

Although this movement away from the Roman Church began as a political one, it soon gathered new support from officials with reforming ideals. The chalice and its central place in the Catholic liturgy was identified by some as part of a religion which had become obsessed with 'pylgremages, worshyppyng off seyntes, wurshypyng off ymages, off purgatory.' These same protesters used the change in religious direction to gain support for their ideals. Although there was a great deal of backing for the process of reformation, which had its roots in previous iconoclastic movements, much of England was still wedded to the traditions and structure of the Catholic Church and were

28. Warden Abbey Morses. Copper-gilt and enamel, England, late 14th century. Diameter 11.8–12 cm. British Museum 1853,0607.1-3.

shocked by some of the wholesale destruction of a religion which was still much loved. Bishop Stephen Gardiner of Winchester claimed in 1547 that:

> 'The images of Christ and his sainctes have ben most contemptuously pulled downe and spitefully handled.'

As the Lacock Cup was presumably held in private hands during this period it would have escaped any attention which was directed by the crown towards the religious establishment. During the revolution under Henry VIII most of the reforming zeal was directed towards monastic institutions, while at a parish level certain areas of the country experienced more destruction than others. It was during the reign of Henry's son Edward VI (1547–1553) that the shape of religion in the English parish would be reformed completely, with particular attention paid towards the altar and its function. Over the years 1547/8 the Mass would be abolished and replaced, the books used during the ceremony were confiscated, the rood screens with their sculptures of the crucifixion were taken down, and the walls with their multicoloured paintings were whitewashed.

29. Iconoclasm
and plunder.
Print on paper,
Franz Hogenberg,
Netherlands, 1566.
20.8 cm x 27.8 cm.
British Museum
1989,0930.167.

Nach wenigh Predication
Die Caluinſche Religion

Das bildenſturmen fiengen an
Das nicht ein bildt dauon bleib ſtan

Kap Mons trantz, kilch, auch die altar   Zerbrochen all in kurtzer s fundt
Vnd weß sonst dort vor handen war,   Gleich gar vil leuten das ist kundt.

From dining table to communion table

The cult of death in late medieval England stimulated the endowment of parish churches, with painted screens, vestments for the clergy and altar cloths. It also prompted the construction of additional chapels and provided the equipment for priests to conduct Mass. Devotion to images were maintained in life and death through the burning of candles in front of saints in memory of the departed. St Cyriac's, Lacock (fig. 30) was no exception. Surviving monuments in the church detail the local noble families within the village at this time. Two notable families with close ties to both the church and the surrounding estates, which have large scale monuments, are the Sharingtons and the Baynards. These are the two most likely families from which the Lacock Cup may have come. The west porch of the church is decorated with a vaulted ceiling, and in the centre of the vault is a shield emblazoned with the arms of the Baynard family (fig. 31). The Baynards held the local manor of Lackham on which the south transept chapel of Saint Cyriac's church was built. This is also where presumably a large brass effigy dating from 1500 of Robert Baynard and his wife, alongside their eleven children, was originally placed. Other notable local families included the Sharingtons, who under William were the first family to take over the dissolved Lacock Abbey, and who refashioned it into their family home. The Sharingtons endowed the building of the sumptuous Lady Chapel, adjacent to the chancel, where the ornate tomb of William still lies (fig. 32). The Baynards played a major role in the church and the parish for many generations. The final Abbess (the female superior) of Lacock Abbey at its suppression was also a member of this family. Although the reigns of the Tudor monarchs were turbulent and changed the face of English religion, they could not alter the fact that active involvement through church donations was a major part of the process of salvation and community interaction at both parish and higher levels. Although we can never

know for certain who gave the Lacock Cup to St Cyriac's, or exactly at which point in history, it can be argued that the most likely candidate came from either of the most prominent local families, the Sharingtons or the Baynards.

Like father like son

Edward VI was particularly zealous in his Protestantism. He suppressed the chantries (buildings dedicated to the singing of masses for the souls of the dead) in 1547 and sold off the buildings, putting an end to a practice which under Henry VI had financed the building of Eton College and Kings College, Cambridge. He introduced the anti-papist Book of Common Prayer in 1549, which advocated the taking of communion only once a year rather than the daily Catholic tradition. His court was Protestant, and in the initial years of his short reign he was guided by the Lord Protector, Edward Seymour, 1st Duke of Somerset, who encouraged a Church populated by individuals such as the Archbishop of Canterbury, Thomas Cranmer and the Bishop of Rochester – then London – Nicholas Ridley. It was Ridley who ordered the destruction of all altars in 1550, replacing them with communion tables, and stated that communion should be administered with a good communion cup of approved Protestant form. The earliest example is held at St Lawrence Jewry, London and is dated to 1548 (not illustrated). Ridley was later, under the reign of Catholic Mary Tudor (1553–58), martyred for his Protestant beliefs.

The confiscation of monastic goods under Henry VIII was echoed at a parish level by Edward in the 1550s. A vast countrywide inventory of church property was undertaken in 1552, with the removal of goods in 1553. St Cyriac's in Lacock features in this account, with silver documented as weighing 20 oz. It has always been assumed that the Lacock Cup could not have been present in the church at this time as it weighs 902 g, taking it beyond the calculations of Edward's surveyors. We cannot however rule out the possibility that the Cup was hidden and therefore not included in the visitation, although moves were made to stop the seclusion or sale of church goods in 1549, policed by sheriffs and Justices of the Peace. To enforce this further, a signature from the warden of the church was required to acknowledge that 'we knowledge ourselves straightly commanded neither to sell nor alienat nor any plate, jewelles, ornamentes or belles from henceforth.' The

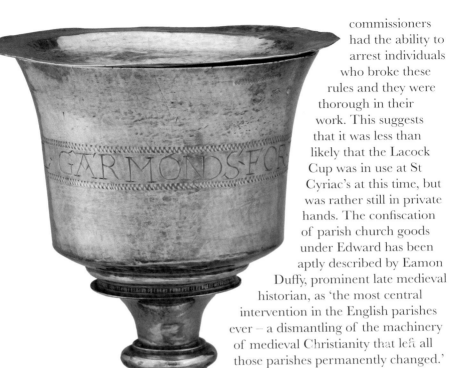

commissioners had the ability to arrest individuals who broke these rules and they were thorough in their work. This suggests that it was less than likely that the Lacock Cup was in use at St Cyriac's at this time, but was rather still in private hands. The confiscation of parish church goods under Edward has been aptly described by Eamon Duffy, prominent late medieval historian, as 'the most central intervention in the English parishes ever – a dismantling of the machinery of medieval Christianity that left all those parishes permanently changed.' The 'good cup' in offical use by the 1550s, represented a major change in the development of the English chalice (fig. 33). In contrast to medieval chalices, it had a short stem and large bowl, similar to the style of the Lacock Cup. These new cups were designed to hold enough wine for the whole congregation, as the laity as well as the clergy could now take Communion in both kinds, both bread and wine. The Eucharist shifted from the altar at the east end of the church, where the chancel once was, to a table in the middle of the nave or crossing. Although we cannot know for certain the actual wealth of medieval silver at St Cyriac's Lacock, we can estimate that for its

33. Wiggenhall St German's Cup. Silver, made by Thomas Buttell, Norwich, 1567–68. Height 16 cm; diameter 10.5 cm. British Museum 1887,0729.2.

size and location, and the splendour of its architectural endowment, it would have been a well-equipped institution. Therefore the destruction and stripping of its altars would have drastically changed the structure, focus and ritual of worship in the church during the sixteenth century. For the Baynards and the Sharingtons, along with the rest of the parish, this must have been a shocking time, regardless of their religious beliefs. It was most certainly a time of great uncertainty and anxiety.

Edward died abruptly in 1553, and was succeeded by his sister, Mary Tudor, who was a committed Catholic. Mary reversed the course of the Reformation and reinstituted the Catholic Mass at the altar. This return was short-lived and would be reversed once more at the succession of her sister Elizabeth I. Elizabeth's reign was long (1558–1603), and through her the English Protestant Church, albeit less radical in reform than from Edward's, became established and the country moved finally away from Rome.

The altar transformed

The Lacock Cup had witnessed the changing fashions of a medieval world which had become a distant memory for the late Tudors. Whoever owned it must have seen it as an important relic of a past and a sense of custom which had long since disappeared. English parish churches under Elizabeth and her successor James I had suffered and they were in a state of disrepair. The ceremony of the Mass had been substituted for that of Communion and without the focus of an altar, or a privileged place for burial in the chancel or the chantry, donations of silver and architectural fabric were less common than they had been previously.

The Sharingtons in Lacock

During the Middle Ages the most powerful local institution in Lacock was the Abbey, situated within walking distance of the church. The Abbess of Lacock held the advowson (the right to appoint the parish priest) for St Cyriac's and had an active role both in the religious and political life of the village community. After the dissolution of the monasteries under Henry VIII, most of these buildings

34. Floor tiles from Lacock Abbey, bearing the heraldry and initials of William Sharington. Lead-glazed earthenware, England, c.1550. Length 12 cm; width 12.8 cm. British Museum 1969,1201.1-2.

were either destroyed, left to ruin, or sold off to private individuals. Lacock Abbey was purchased by William Sharington in 1539, who made vast alterations to the fabric of the estate, transforming the site from a place dedicated to religious life into a private house. Under the new system, Sharington inherited the patronage of St Cyriac's from the Abbess of Lacock. The church would have been his place of worship and his connection to the building is established by his splendid tomb, carved from stone with heraldry that matches floor tiles which once decorated the newly transformed Lacock Abbey (fig. 34).

Sharington was not well liked in Lacock, and there is evidence that he was not totally adept at his new role as patron of St Cyriac's. However his position locally and his financial commitment to the church make him a prime candidate as the donor of the Lacock Cup. Silver and gold objects donated to churches in the seventeenth and eighteenth centuries often bear inscriptions announcing the name of the individual associated with the donation. The Lacock Cup has no such inscription, although this is not a clear sign of the date of its donation. It does however mean that the donor did not see it as necessary, or that it was not common, to have an inscription added as a mark of remembrance. As has already been suggested, the Cup is stylistically similar to the type of cup manufactured in the middle of the sixteenth century for the communion table. A particularly similar example is held at St Mary Aldermary, London (fig. 35). It it entirely possible that William Sharington donated the Cup to St Cyriac's, which in the sixteenth century might have been found without a suitable communion cup in the change of liturgy from Henry VIII to Edward VI, or from Mary to Elizabeth I. Sharington's financial involvement meant that he would have been one of the first individuals the church would have turned to when in need of help. However, as Sharington was not well liked and his relationship with the church was not always a smooth one, the other notable family in the area must sit alongside his as a contender for donor of the Cup.

The Baynards of Lackham

As has been previously described the Baynards were a historic local family with close ties to the church and village. Parish churches in England during the sixteenth century entered a state of flux, however in the first half of the seventeenth century, something interesting began to happen. In 1623 two monuments were erected at St Cyriac's by Sir Robert Baynard – one to his father Edward, the other to his wife Ursula. On 12th November 1629 the chancel in the church of St Cyriac's was repaired. On 16th October 1632 a burial is recorded as taking place in the chancel. In 1635 stairs are added to the church by its patron, Dame Olive Stapleton, to aid passage to the organ. In 1637 a silver paten is donated for use in the church and is inscribed with the name of the donor, Susan Salway. Then, on 7th April 1640, repairs were undertaken once again. What at first seems to be a list of routine alterations is rather more enlightening. Clearly efforts were being made to reorder and revitalize the appearance of the church. During the preceding generations many churches had lost their organs, the chancels had become dilapidated spaces and monuments associated with burial were not allowed in the chancel. In the reign of Charles I (1625–49), as the persecutions of Protestants under Mary, and Catholics under Elizabeth became a distant memory, things began to change. Between the years 1620–40, the Church of England saw a renewed interest in the replacement of altars and the reinstatement of certain composed liturgical practices. By the end of the 1630s several publications on the redecoration and rebuilding of churches had been published, the most famous being *De Templis: A Treatise of Temples, wherein is discovered the Ancient Manner of Building, Consecrating and Adorning Churches.* This book advocated the placement of the altar in the chancel at the east end of the church and stated that 'Hither bring your stateliest hanging, and adorne the walls; hither your richest carpets, and bespread the ground; hither the most glorious silke and finest linen, to cover the Holy Table.'

A central figure in this movement was William Laud, who in 1633 became the Archbishop of Canterbury. Laud was a great reformer of the church, and believed in the beautifying of church interiors. He took his inspiration from Psalm 96:9 which insisted that you should 'worship the Lord in holy splendour.' Under Laud a wave of enthusiastic church decoration took place, which touched not only the physical appearance of the church and its chancel but also the literature of devotion and the music to accompany the ceremonies. Candlesticks, cloth and even some crosses were to be found in churches, however most crucial was the advocation of a fine chalice for the taking of Holy Communion.

Returning to the two monuments commissioned by Sir Robert Baynard, a closer analysis of these and the family gives tantalizing insight into a possible origin for the Lacock Cup. Sir Robert's father and wife did not die in the same year, however at the death of his wife, Ursula, he must have considered it appropriate to commission a monument to both relatives. These memorials not only mention the living qualities of those commemorated, but they also document their pedigree. Both monuments are adorned with painted heraldic shields, providing an ancient lineage. The church was already a monument to the family, but through the fifteenth-century heraldry the Baynards gained a deeper sense of presence at St Cyriac's. Sadly Ursula's monument records the birth of Edward, the only son born to her and Robert, who died before his third birthday. Although there were other living Baynards, Sir Robert's estate did not pass on to a male heir, but changed families at the marriage of his daughter to a Montagu. The death of his family, and indeed his name, must have been present in his thoughts and actions as Sir Robert commissioned these monuments. Only two years previously his mother, Margaret Monpassant, passed away, leaving to her son in her will of 1621 'the wedding ring I had of his father...and one broad cuppe of silver parcel guilte'. It is impossible to know whether or not the cup mentioned in her will is the Lacock Cup. However, it is possible, given the building of the monuments in Saint Cyriac's Church, and the practice of beautifying churches under Archbishop Laud, that between 1621, when Robert inherits a cup, and 1636, upon his death, that the Lacock Cup was given to the church. It is perhaps significant that no cup of the sort he inherited was recorded in the inventory of his possessions at his death.

If Sir Robert Baynard had owned the Cup, he might have given it to the church in memory of his mother, and may have donated it in agreement with the reforms of Laud and his contemporaries – perhaps believing that it was a fine addition to enrich the altar. As we know, Sir Robert was the last male heir of the Baynard estate, and after his death it passed to his daughter. As Sir Robert approached his death, and looked at the church documenting the history of the Baynards, might he have thought of giving the Cup to mark the end of the male line in his family, or to look for the beginning of a new life in Heaven?

Village life and beyond

Although we cannot be certain that the Lacock Cup was donated in the late 1500s or early 1600s, by the Baynards or the Sharingtons, the two centuries following the Reformation are the most likely in which such a gift would have been valued and preserved. It happened to be in the right place at the right time. Following the Laudian reforms of the early seventeenth century, the Church of England was again thrown into a period of instability during the English Civil War (1642–1651), and Oliver Cromwell's subsequent rule. Cromwell rejected the changes made by Laud and Charles I, and under him a new wave of iconoclasm and confiscations began. The survival of Susan Salway's donated paten shows that pre-revolution silver was protected within the parish, and the Lacock Cup most likely survived with it. By the late nineteenth and early twentieth centuries, the Cup, the paten and a flagon donated in 1701, constituted the antique silverware of the church, and were treasured as such (fig. 36).

The twentieth century brought the Lacock Cup into public view in a very different way, through its inclusion in publications and exhibitions. An object of great beauty, its importance must have always been apparent, to those in the parish, when it was used in the church, and as has been shown through church surveys of the nineteenth century, the Cup was often singled out as a treasure of Wiltshire. However over the years its history was lost. It was only in the twentieth century that the historical importance of the Cup was realized. In 1937 and 1955 the Cup made two trips to exhibitions (*Treasures of the West Country* and *Silver Treasures from English Churches* respectively), the first at Bristol, and the latter at Christie's in London for the Historic Churches Preservation Trust. The 1955 exhibition catalogue described it as an 'extremely rare and interesting cup.' Following a loan to Vienna in 1962, for the exhibition *European Art around 1400*, the lending of the Cup was agreed to the British Museum by the Keeper of the Department of British and Medieval Antiquities, R.L.S. Bruce-Mitford, and the Rector the Reverend Mr. G.R. Brocklebank. There was, however, a surprising clause to the loan, that the Cup would travel

back to Lacock from London Paddington to be met by a 'responsible person of the parish' for use, four times a year, at Christmas, Easter, Whitsun and Harvest. We can assume that the Cup was historically associated with use on these important festivals, as a report to the Trustees of the British Museum dated 26th September 1962, notes that: 'the parish is accumstomed to using the Cup as a communion chalice on four occasions during the year and would wish to continue to do so'. Apart from church treasuries it is extremely rare for a museum object to move from display to public use, and yet the Lacock Cup did so, well into the twentieth century, which again is testament to the high-esteem in which the Cup was held.

After twenty years on loan to the British Museum, the transporting of the Cup back to St Cyriac's became untenable for insurance reasons. From this point the Cup was looked after by the British Museum, where it has been on permanent display ever since. The Cup was acquired by the Museum in December 2013. As a mark of recognition of the importance of the Cup to the history and community of St Cyriac's, the British Museum has commissioned a facsimile, made by it's own expert craftsman, which will continue to have a role in the life of the church into the twenty-first century.

Acknowledgements

The authors would like to thank John Cherry, Dora Thornton, Roger Bland, Becky Allen and Michael Lewis for their careful reading and advice on the text; Saul Peckham for photography; Sue La Niece for scientific testing; John Catchpole from St Cyriac's, Lacock for his unending support; the Staff of Wilshire and Swindon History Centre; James Robinson for advice and guidance; Axelle Russo-Heath for sourcing the images; Kate Oliver for her production expertise; and finally Emma Poulter for her careful editing.

The Lacock Cup was jointly acquired by the British Museum and the Wiltshire Museum with the support of the National Heritage Memorial Fund, John Studzinski, the Art Fund, the American Friends of the British Museum, the British Museum Friends, the Jean Sibley Bequest, the Charity Fund of International Partners Limited in memory of Melvin R. Seiden, Howard and Roberta Ahmanson, the Headley Trust and individual contributions.

NATIONAL
HERITAGE
MEMORIAL
FUND

Further reading

M. Campbell, 'Gold, silver and precious stones', in
   J. Blair & N. Ramsay (eds), *English Medieval Industries:*
   Craftsmen, Techniques, Products, London, 1991, pp. 107–166

J. Cherry, *Medieval Goldsmiths*, London, 2011

E. Duffy, *Stripping of the the Altars: Traditional Religion in England*
   1400–1580, Yale, 2005

K. Fincham & N. Tyacke, *Altars Restored: The Changing Face of*
   English Religious Worship, 1547–c.1700, Oxford, 2007

P. Glanville, *Silver in England*, London, 1987

P. Glanville, *Silver in Tudor and Early Stuart England*, London,
   1997

A.G. Grimwade, *Catalogue of Silver Treasures from English*
   Churches: An Exhibition of Ecclesiastical Plate of Domestic Origin,
   exh. cat., Christie's, London, 1955

C. J. Jackson, *An illustrated history of English plate, ecclesiastical*
   and secular, in which the development of form and decoration in
   the silver and gold work of the British Isles from the earliest known
   examples to the latest of the Georgian period is delineated and
   described, 2 vols, London, 1911

R. Marks & P Williamson (eds), *Gothic: Art for England 1400–*
   1547, exh. cat., London, 2003

C. Oman, *English Church Plate 597–1830*, London, 1957

G. Parry, *Glory, Laud and Honour: The Arts of the Counter-*
   Reformation, Woodbridge, 2008

T. B. Schroder (ed.), *Treasures of the English Church: A Thousand*
   Years of Sacred Gold & Silver, London, 2008

For a wider history of the county of Wiltshire, see the
Wiltshire, Victoria County History series.